# I Am Better Than Average

*101 Affirmations*
*to Help You Build and Live*
*A Better Than Average Life*

**by**
**Jonathan McMillan**

Thank you for purchasing this book.

If you enjoyed and benefited from the information contained inside, please recommend it to your friends and family who you would like to be inspired to build and live their own better than average lives. Remember to check with your local bookstore, library and online book retailers to discover other works by Jonathan McMillan.



Thank you for your support.

This book is dedicated to my parents Charles and Judy and my grandparents Omell McMillan, Chester and Hattie Garland who believed I was better than average from day one and even when I didn't believe it or act like it.

Your continued faith in me and support during my lowest and darkest times are is what eventually inspired me to have an introspective examination and begin to develop into the man you all were confident I would always be.

You all are as much authors of this book as I am, for these pages recycle the wisdom you passed on to me over the years in your attempts to affirm me into reaching my potential and achieving the success that has always been my birthright and within my power.

You are my better than average ancestors and I am your better than average legacy.

With Love, Gratitude and Peace, I present the fruits of your labor

- Jo'Natan

# Table of Contents

# Introduction

About four years ago I was fighting for my life.

I had been falsely accused of a horrific crime and was facing a lifetime sentence in prison if convicted.

I decided that I wasn't going to allow that accusation and possible guilty verdict to define my legacy. I decided to create and live my life to the fullest and to the best of my capabilities.

In order to do that, I could not, under any circumstance, allow my thinking to give in to the negativity of the world and lose hope.

Too many times, we defeat ourselves with the negative self-talk that convinces us it's okay to feel sorry for ourselves. We fool ourselves into thinking that playing the role of victim is empowering. The average person's self talk convinces them it's okay to simply be average and to be satisfied with few insignificant accomplishments to show as the sum of their time on this planet. The average person feels no obligation to make any contribution to the world around them and lives in a perpetual state of unawareness of how much they potentially impact those around him or her.

I am, as anyone who is reading these words is, capable

of more and better so I committed to coaching myself to realize that level of achievement just like Phil Jackson did for Michael Jordan and Shaq and Kobe Bryant.

I realized early on, in order to win the fight against the negative, self defeating thoughts, I would have to replace the unproductive, destructive idle mind chatter with deliberate powerfully empowering no nonsense self talk. Words that reminded me of how powerful I am and that it is my right to be the person who fulfills my potential and lives a life of abundance.

So I turned up my level of awareness of my what my subconscious thoughts and self-talk were saying and steered the conversation in the direction which I wanted; empowerment.

About the same time all of this was going on, a friend was going through a fight for her life with breast cancer. She mentioned that some of the things I was posting on Facebook encouraged her and kept her spirits up. She suggested I post something in the spirit of being better than average daily so I started a Facebook group. I would mostly post uplifting and inspirational articles, videos and personal development tips that I found elsewhere online.

Occasionally, I would post my original thoughts in the

form of my empowering self-talk. I wanted to share the things that were encouraging me with those, like my friend who were fighting whatever battle life had brought to them. Eventually, those posts took on the form of the affirmations you'll soon see in this book.

These affirmations are designed to focus your thoughts on the person you intend to be and plan to be. They are powerful tools to train your thinking to be goal oriented and grateful. They are also are tools to help you build the person - mind, body and soul through idealizing, visualizing, and emotionalizing who you desire to be. They can create a clarity in your purpose and renew and support your commitment to that purpose.

Using these affirmations and eventually creating your own will manifest what you need: wisdom, peace and health in abundance in your life when you need it.

Every BTA affirmation begins with the empowering phrase "I am better than average because..."

This is very intentional because the words "I am" are two of the most empowering or destructive words a person can even think let alone utter aloud. Those words form the lens through which one sees their place in world and sets the scale on which one measures their self worth. Action follows identity. In other words, if a person defines themselves as a loser or a victim they will act accordingly and never do the things required to win or be anything other than a victim. Therefore, in order to be successful and achieve anything significant it is imperative that you deliberately and specifically define who you are to yourself.

I choose the term “better than average” not as a judgement of others but as a standard of living and as a rhetorical place where the things I desire spiritually, mentally, physically, financially reside. There are many things that the average person is, does or doesn’t do and is satisfied with. That may be just fine for them, but not me and not for you either.

The better than average affirmations train our minds, tune our spirits and prepare our bodies to do what is necessary to create and live a better than average life.

The affirmations in this book are sorted into five different themes which align with the defining characteristics of a person described as being better than average. I’ve separated these themes into chapters.

At the beginning of each chapter I speak to what the following theme will be and what the overarching subject of that particular chapter is. As such, some of the affirmations may seem repetitive and redundant however, as Muhammad Ali once said, "*It's the repetition of affirmations that leads to belief. And once that belief becomes a deep conviction, things begin to happen.*"

It is my goal that through the affirmations shared in this book you will find or gain inspiration to believe that you are better than average and develop that belief into a conviction so deep that you organically begin to create and live a better than average life.

Chapter One:

# I Am Better Than Average Because I Am Grateful

Gratitude saved me. I was lowest, darkest point of my life when I was facing the criminal charges. I was having difficulty finding any pleasure or appreciating anything, even the abundance of fulfilled necessities and luxuries I possessed. I had a roof over my head and shoes on my feet, food in my stomach and loving relationships surrounding and supporting me.

I even had access to one of the most talented and expensive attorneys in my state thanks to my father's belief in my innocence.

It was once I came to the realization that, with my future so uncertain, I needed to be more appreciative of all that I had now, while I still could.

I challenged myself to express gratitude at least 17 times per day. Almost immediately, my demeanor and circumstances began to improve. My outlook on life brightened and I became hopeful, even confident in my future. I began to notice and take advantage of opportunities to create and live a fulfilling life overflowing with achievements, meaningful relationships and happiness.

It became very evident that the more grateful I was for absolutely everything which was in my life I was drawing on the necessary energy to create and attract more into my life for which I could be grateful.

And that was the beginning of me building and living a better than average life.

# Affirmation Number 1
# I am better than average because:

*I know, believe in and practice the power of gratitude.*

The possibility of the existence of a better than average life depends not on what I do or have but depends, rather, on what I am. In order to be in tune with and operate on the Universal frequencies which holds the energy that manifests a better than average life, I must be absolutely, deliberately, and powerfully grateful for every person, experience, opportunity, and circumstance which I may encounter.

Furthermore, when I act upon that gratitude, I manipulate that energy and attract more into my life for which I am grateful and that process is the natural creation and living of a better than average life.

## Affirmation Number 2
## I am better than average because:

*I am habitually, purposefully and powerfully grateful for every person, experience, opportunity, and circumstance which I encounter, without exception or qualification.*

There is value in the lessons taught by even that which is unpleasant. This paradigm of gratitude which focuses my perception and presence, is the single most important tool in creating and living a better than average life.

## Affirmation Number 3
## I am better than average because:

*I am grateful.*

*I am present.*

These states of being focus me on the people, opportunities, challenges and solutions that make life, literally, an unforgettable experience worth living.

## Affirmation Number 4
## I am better than average because:

*I am especially grateful for*

*disappointments, challenges and failures.*

The quality of character that is built and the lessons that are taught by overcoming these things inevitably make me stronger and wiser and therefore more valuable.

I recycle the negativity which life sometimes presents into the material with which a better than average life is built.

## Affirmation Number 5
## I am better than average because:

*My perspective on life is based in gratitude. The things I focus on increase so I direct my attention and energy toward all that for which I am grateful. This includes the abundance of opportunities, possibilities, inspiration, encouragement, counsel, support, love, health and wealth.*

Paying attention and giving appreciation to the things that create a better than average life is the price I gladly pay to build and live a better than average life.

## Affirmation Number 6
## I am better than average because:

*I view my life from a perspective of immense abundance and powerful, deliberate gratitude.*

*Whatever is mine to give, I do generously, unafraid of scarcity. What is mine to receive I do so gratefully, understanding I will always have enough.*

This paradigm empowers me to view the opportunities and possibilities upon which a better than average life is built.

## Affirmation Number 7
## I am better than average because:

*I pay attention to all that I have for which I am grateful.*

In return, I am rewarded with abundantly more. I direct my focus on the good in and around me which magnifies its presence and amplifies its power to create and live a better than average life.

## Affirmation Number 8
## I am better than average because:

*I am aware that scarcity, poverty, lack and illness are conditions which can only affect me if I accept to them.*

These conditions are states of mind more than states of being - which can be deliberately be cured and changed by intentional changes in thoughts, beliefs, emotions and behavior.

I live a better than average life built on a foundation of awareness and gratitude of the abundance of wealth, health, opportunity and empowering, inspirational relationships that exist.

## Affirmation Number 9
## I am better than average because:

*I am grateful for all of my experiences, both good and bad. They contribute to my understanding and growth therefore they made me who I am.*

Absolute, unconditional gratitude is the energy that creates more experiences that magnify the goodness that the Universe has to offer and transforms the negative into learning opportunities. It is the stage upon which a better than average life performs for those who desire to create and live it out.

## Affirmation Number 10
## I am better than average because:

*I get to choose what type of day I am going to have. I am excited about all I get to do. I am grateful for the possibilities and opportunities to create and live a better than average life full of great days.*

I chose to build and live a better than average life. Choice is the ultimate expression of freedom and power especially when it comes to one's mindset and emotions. The average person usually fails to realize how many choices they have and thus fails to recognize how much freedom and power they have over their conditions and circumstances whether they be financial, physical, social, emotional or mental.

## Affirmation Number 11
## I am better than average because:

*I choose the freeway of gratitude over the crowded streets of complaint.*

This is the only route which leads to the success and the only one which makes the journey as enjoyable as the destination.

The road of gratitude is paved with opportunity, possibility, and celebration and is a direct shortcut to a better than average life.

## Affirmation Number 12
## I am better than average because:

*I am in tune with and operate at the frequency of gratitude.*

I challenge myself to to be so present and aware of all that I have, both now and in the future, that my state of consciousness becomes habitual, purposeful, powerful gratitude which is where a better than average life is born and thrives.

## Affirmation Number 13
## I am better than average because:

*No matter my current circumstances, I exercise the right and the power to improve my condition by simply practicing deliberate, powerful gratitude.*

*This doesn't mean that I am not bothered by unpleasant people and situations. It simply means I do not allow my current or future happiness to be controlled or metered by choosing to focus on unpleasantness.*

This ability and freedom to be unconditionally grateful is the fabric of a better than average life.

## Affirmation Number 14
## I am better than average because:

*My gratitude is limitless because I have clearly defined my wants versus my needs.*

*My needs are simply the things required to live life: air, food, shelter and a functional mind.*

*My wants are the things which makes living that life a worthwhile experience like, wealth, material possessions, significant relationships and whatever success I have set as my goals.*

I have few needs, I have all that I need, I have more than I need and I may have anything which my actions confirm I want. The belief and understanding that there is no ceiling on opportunities for me to experience gratitude is the foundation to build a better than average life and the magnets attracting all that I desire as I live that life.

## Affirmation Number 15
## I am better than average because:

*I inspire and lead others to create and live their own better than average lives by powerfully, deliberately and habitually demonstrating gratitude toward every person, circumstance and opportunity which I encounter.*

By aspiring to inspire others, I ensure that I am creating and living my own better than average life on purpose and by example.

## Affirmation Number 16
## I am better than average because:

*I am not discouraged by nor am I influenced by the negativity of the world. I do not contribute to the negativity.*

While the average person gives energy and calls attention to that which is upsetting and disappointing, I direct my focus and spend my energy on finding and creating solutions and opportunities for the world and I to experience gratitude.

## Affirmation Number 17
## I am better than average because:

*I powerfully, deliberately and habitually exercise gratitude by routinely asking myself two questions:*

1. *What are you feeling at this very moment?*
2. *Where are you focusing your energy?*

The only acceptable answers are

1. "Grateful".

and

2. on creating opportunities for myself and others to experience gratitude."

This strengthening of presence, self awareness and commitment is what builds a better than average life for myself and others.

## Affirmation Number 18
## I am better than average because:

*I create gratitude.*

Even when I have trouble finding the good in the world, that is when I focus on the good I can and should create for myself and others.

This willingness to act is the obligation to which I must agree in order to create and live a better than average life.

## Affirmation Number 19
## I am better than average because:

*I create and then focus on my gratitude for that which I don't even have yet as motivation to do what is necessary to receive it.*

Gratitude is the limitless energy which fuels the work required to create and then live a better than average life.

## Affirmation Number 20
## I am better than average because:

*I do not allow my desire for the things I don't currently possess to overwhelm my gratitude for all that I do have.*

*I recognize my few needs are sufficiently met and I have an abundance of opportunity, possibilities and means to obtain all that I want.*

Gratitude is the substance of a better than average life which will always tip the scale of abundance to my advantage.

## Affirmation Number 21
## I am better than average because:

*I create happiness and prosperity by viewing life from a perspective of gratitude.*

Whereas the average person seeks happiness by pursuing that which they perceive they lack, I constantly enjoy the peace that comes from seeing and recognizing the abundance which exists in the present and the limitless prosperity on the horizon which only I have the ability to manifest for myself.

This grateful frame of reference is that which transforms the canvas of life into a better than average masterpiece.

## Affirmation Number 22
## I am better than average because:

*I am grateful even in the face of adversity.*

*It is especially during difficult times that I manage my emotions, dictate my mood and encourage myself and others through practicing the habit of being powerfully and deliberately grateful for every person, opportunity, and circumstance which I encounter.*

Challenging myself to be unconditionally aware of all that I have, currently and in the future is the action which transforms the terrain of the mind, where a better than average life is built, from hostile to habitable.

Chapter Two

# I Am Destined for Greatness

Destiny is a combination of a desire to achieve a certain goal, a belief that you are able and deserve to achieve that goal and willingness to do what is required to achieve that goal.

Because we have determined ourselves to be better than average, by extension, the goals we set for ourselves are also better than average. I mention this because whether you know it or not, the achievement of those goals are acts of greatness.

The term greatness is 100% personal and subjective. To some, it may mean celebrity, fame and wealth. To others it may mean being incredibly uplifting and inspiring nations and generations of people to raise up and overcome. And still, to others, greatness may simply mean doing what they expect of themselves and creating and living a fulfilled life. For example, greatness may be starting that small business you've always dreamed about or graduating from high school at the top of your class or being the devoted, loving parent to your children that you never experienced.

This chapter is dedicated to the better than average goals, better than average focus and better than average routines necessary to create and live out one's destiny of a better than average life.

## Affirmation Number 23
## I am better than average because:

*I know that I am destined for success because I have the desire to succeed, the belief in my right and ability to succeed and the willingness to do whatever is necessary to achieve success.*

Destiny is oftentimes mistaken for fate which is uncontrollable and unchangeable. The fact of the matter is: destiny is like clay which is precisely shaped by the of the thoughts, actions and character of the person who holds it. Therefore, success and greatness are inevitable outcomes of focused desire, unwavering belief and unrelenting willingness to do what is required to achieve it.

## Affirmation Number 24
## I am better than average because:

*I know, undoubtedly, where I intend to be so I march forward in that direction with commitment and conviction - never allowing obstacles or detours to diminish my determination to reach my destination but rather fortify it until it matures into the same natural purpose that compels me take my next breath.*

Creating and living a better than average life is my natural purpose, same as eating, sleeping and any and every other natural drive of my human condition. The same way I'm driven to fulfill those compulsions, I relentlessly march toward achieving the greatness that is my destined purpose.

## Affirmation Number 25
## I am better than average because:

*I believe that I absolutely deserve whatever success I have set my sight on. I know that my birthright and destiny is greatness.*

From the moment I was born I was given the power to create new preferred circumstances and status and replace of any old condition. I have the right and power to bring forth something new and better for myself. Every new day is an opportunity to create and live a better than average life.

## Affirmation Number 26
## I am better than average because:

*I know almost any goal- no matter how difficult - can be made attainable with proper planning.*

The creating and living of a better than average life doesn't happen by accident; It is planned.

Proper planning only requires identifying three things:

1. Obstacles I must overcome.
2. Knowledge, skills and habits I must possess to overcome those obstacles.
3. People whose help I'll need in order to obtain that knowledge or those skills and habits.

## Affirmation Number 27
## I am better than average because:

*I know my purpose is ultimately to be happy.*

My thoughts are managed, my actions are deliberate and my relationships are designed to build and live a better than average life which naturally creates the happiness that most people pursue.

## Affirmation Number 28
## I am better than average because:

*I view my pursuit of success as I do breathing.*

*I do not hesitate to take my next breath as it is necessary to continue to live.*

*Likewise, I do not procrastinate when taking the initiative toward doing whatever steps are necessary for my goals to be achieved.*

*If I pause, my dreams, goals and ambitions expire.*

Creating a better than average life is my purpose. Living a better than average life through consistent thoughts, words and deeds, is my destiny.

## Affirmation Number 29
## I am better than average because:

*I clearly visualize achieving my goals.*

I have a detailed picture in my mind of what a better than average life looks like and how it's built and lived. That clear picture gives me greater energy and motivates me to exert maximum effort toward making it a reality faster.

## Affirmation Number 30
## I am better than average because:

*I set my goals based on what I (and only I) have idealized my life to be.*

I don't apply limits to my dreams or goals based on what anyone else's opinion or doubts of what what is or isn't possible.

The building and living a better than average life is defined 100% by my standards and commitment to do so.

## Affirmation Number 31
## I am better than average because:

*I choose to focus on my opportunity and potential rather than limitation and impossibility.*

The things I focus on expand and increase. Opportunities, solutions, abundance, health, wealth, career, productive relationships and all the things that create a better than average life. Focusing on those things daily is the starting point of creating and living a better than average life.

## Affirmation Number 32
## I am better than average because:

*I plan my day precisely in order to be more productive than distracted.*

I know what I expect to have accomplished by the end of my day and by certain deadlines throughout. This allows me to stay focused and a steadily create and live a better than average life full of achievements both big and small.

## Affirmation Number 33
## I am better than average because:

*I am disciplined.*

I do what I must even if it isn't ideal or doesn't result in immediate gratification. My discipline is one of the most important tools I have at my disposal to build a better than average life which I then live by reaping the rewards of that discipline.

## Affirmation Number 34
## I am better than average because:

*I know the most powerful or destructive tools at my disposal are the habits which I routinely exercise.*

Whether mentally, emotionally, intellectually, financially, spiritually, or physically, I consciously and subconsciously constantly and consistently behave in a manner which helps me build and live a better than average life.

## Affirmation Number 35
## I am better than average because:

*I am consistent.*

I rise early, daily, to not just face my challenges, obstacles, and adversaries, but to soundly defeat them and achieve my goals even if my only means of winning is by wearing them down slowly and gradually.

Success is the result of consistent, constant efforts which become habits. The building and living a better than average life is practicing success as a lifestyle.

## Affirmation Number 36
## I am better than average because:

*I can and will do what is necessary to succeed.*

I don’t just do what is comfortable, like blaming others for setbacks and temporary failures.

I create and own my agenda and take responsibility for my success through admission of, but not surrender to failure. I then analyze and learn from my mistakes. By committing to do my best and to get better when my best isn’t good enough, I create and live a better than average life.

## Affirmation Number 37
## I am better than average because:

*I identify obstacles (especially internal ones) I will have to overcome and plan accordingly by constantly developing the necessary skills and habits to consistently progress, accomplish, produce, and succeed.*

A better than average life is built and lived through setting and achieving goals. Almost any and every goal can be accomplished by not running from or ignoring the obstacles which naturally exist but rather by identifying them and developing a plan which consists of becoming skilled and disciplined enough to overcome them.

## Affirmation Number 38
## I am better than average because:

*I understand that the majority of obstacles that I must overcome in order to be successful and achieve my goals are internal.*

*They are the characteristics and thinking and emotional habits which limit my chances of success.*

Identifying these characteristics in my life helps me to understand exactly where I need to begin my journey toward being the type of person who creates and lives a better than average life.

## Affirmation Number 39
## I am better than average because:

*My view is not at the level of the challenge but the level of possibility. I move my awareness away from the level of obstacles to the level of divine potential always present.*

When I focus on my birthright and my power to improve my condition and circumstances am encouraged and energized to do what is required in order to do so. I set large goals, implement precise plans to accomplish them and develop the necessary skills, habits and relationships that execute those plans. This process is quite simply the building and living a better than average life.

## Affirmation Number 40
## I am better than average because:

*When it comes to obstacles delaying me achieving my goals, I only acknowledge them long enough to identify them. I then immediately focus on finding or creating solutions by developing the necessary skills, habits and social network that facilitate my success.*

The understanding that solutions, opportunities and unlimited potential for success is abundant is the mindset that allows me to create and live a better than average life.

## Affirmation Number 41
## I am better than average because:

*I know my weakest key skill/worst habit sets the ceiling of my potential success so I ask myself two crucial questions:*

1. *What one skill or habit if properly developed would help me the most?*
2. *What daily habit would set me on the path toward success as a lifestyle?*

A better than average life is simultaneously created and lived by concentrating on developing and improving skills and habits which overcome obstacles. This is the process that creates potential for success.

## Affirmation Number 42
## I am better than average because:

*I have clarity when it comes to acting upon my goals that comes from having a plan. I know the difference between what I can do, should do, must do and what I am willing to do.*

Many times we are confused as to where we should focus our energy so we end up wasting much of it acting in ways which don't advance our goals. Identifying what needs to be done, planning the required steps and focusing the necessary energy are all simple steps in building and living better than average lives.

## Affirmation Number 43
## I am better than average because:

*I free myself from mental limitations and perceived barriers that slow my progress by focusing on my right and power to tap into the abundance of possibility and opportunity available to me . These limitations are fear, feelings of inferiority and unworthiness, resentments and grudges and an unwillingness to be uncomfortable.*

The road to a better than average life has obstacles but none which are insurmountable with a commitment to developing the necessary skills, habits, support network and a better than average mindset.

The average person spends too much time and energy focusing on their fears of failure, poverty and other negative factors rather than what they truly want out of life or what they need to do in order to get it. By remaining focused on the better than average life that is within my power to create and which is my birthright to live, I am sure to increase opportunities and resources to overcome obstacles.

## Affirmation Number 44
## I am better than average because:

*I view life through a paradigm of an victor not victim.*

The average person defines themselves by the events that happen to them rather than the events which they overcame. They focus on the few things which they have no control over rather than all the abundance of opportunity, possibilities and power they have to create and live a better than average life for themselves as victors, survivors, and winners.

Chapter Three

# I Am Better Than Average Because I Embrace Change

Change is inevitable. From one second to the next countless things are different than they were the moment before. The average person denies and fights against this unwavering fact of existence creating hostility and turmoil. You can focus on the benefits of change and by embracing and managing it and then be empowered to direct your time and energy towards creating and living a better than average life for yourself and others.

## Affirmation Number 45
## I am better than average because:

*I embrace change because I know and accept that it is a sometimes difficult but always necessary part of growth.*

My ultimate goal, living a better than average life, is, at its core, change.

Changing my ways of thinking, feeling, and behaving is achieving that goal by creating the life I want to live.

## Affirmation Number 46
## I am better than average because:

*I know and accept the fact that change is inevitable. I also know when change is properly managed it can be extremely rewarding.*

This is the better than average perspective that keeps me focused on the possibilities rather than the difficulties when processing the necessary changes I must make in my current condition and circumstances. Change is the goal when identifying the obstacles I must overcome, the skills and habits I must develop and the relationships I must leave and/or create in order to create and live a better than average life.

## Affirmation Number 47
## I am better than average because:

*I focus on what I gain-- not lose as I make necessary changes to my lifestyle and habits in order to create and live a better than averaged life.*

Managed, purposeful change makes me more valuable because I gain new experiences, lessons and strengths.

These are the very ingredients that compose a better than average life.

## Affirmation Number 48
## I am better than average because:

*I do not wallow in misery.*

*The level of my happiness is only restricted by my commitment to be happy and my willingness to find and create happiness, peace and solutions to obstacles.*

An unwavering commitment to happiness is a contract with the Universe agreeing to build and live a better than average life.

## Affirmation Number 49
## I am better than average because:

*An indestructible positive mindset is an essential tool for creating a better than average life.*

I create and strengthen a better than average mindset through mindful presence and consistent self evaluation.

During those moments when I catch my consciousness on autopilot and my thoughts wandering aimlessly, I refocus myself by asking "Are my thoughts, feelings and behavior where they need to be to in order to live a better than average life?" and then I adjust accordingly.

## Affirmation Number 50
## I am better than average because:

*I only form an opinion after engaging in independent, critical thinking.*

*I am confident and unafraid to share my thoughts on any subject on which I have thoroughly, objectively educated myself but even then, I only share my opinion if it is inspiring, encouraging, and motivating to others.*

My right to express an opinion, no matter how well informed rarely outweighs the benefit of peace that comes from practicing self restraint and simply doing what is right.

A better than average life is built by action inspired by focused prosperous thoughts, not trivial chatter or ego driven arguments.

## Affirmation Number 51
## I am better than average because:

*I act upon my convictions.*

In an era where technology has reduced activism to meme creation, post liking and re-sharing, and hashtags, the average person is only as passionate about their individual causes as their comfort zone allows which is why the status quo is rarely affected.

I am committed to putting in maximum effort towards creating change in those matters which profoundly affect or concern me, most of which is building and living a better than average life.

This most certainly requires actually acting intentionally and engaging with the world in ways which are often times uncomfortable, unpopular, uncertain and uneasy.

## Affirmation Number 52
## I am better than average because:

*I operate at a frequency that is higher than self-pity.*

This makes it possible for me to tune out those who broadcast that negativity and other negative energies and allows me to synchronize my thoughts, emotions and actions with the energy which fuels a better than average life.

# Affirmation Number 53
# I am better than average because:

*I refuse to be a slave to anger and sadness.*

Victims choose to focus on these emotions because they are easy, common and familiar even though they serve no purpose.

I direct my thoughts and behaviors to move closer to my desired emotional state and purposely distance myself from thinking, things, people, actions and habits which do not contribute to my peace and happiness which is the ultimate measure of a better than average life.

# Affirmation Number 54
# I am better than average because:

*My emotions motivate me rather than control me.*

I do not operate or make decisions out of the base emotions of fear and anger nor allow any emotion to override my intellect. I don't think, speak or behave negatively or destructively just because I'm mad or sad, insecure or in a similar emotional state.

I deliberately think, say and do what is required to find or create peace and happiness which is the foundation upon which a better than average life of built.

## Affirmation Number 55
## I am better than average because:

*I am able to, and do, choose my disposition regardless of my circumstances.*

I have the right and power to create better for myself. However, in order to do so I must exercise those same rights and powers internally and take complete responsibility for how I show up in the world and treat others regardless of external, uncontrollable conditions or internal turmoil. This mindset and self-control exercise is a magnet which attracts the positive energy and relationships which help me create and live a better than average life.

## Affirmation Number 56
## I am better than average because:

*I do not allow my emotions to override my intellect.*

I do not excuse behavior that is detrimental to me accomplishing my goals by handing the reigns of my life over to negative emotions such as anger, fear or sadness.

I realize it is my duty to control my emotions and gain access to abundant opportunities, positivity, wealth, health and all that contributes to the building and living a better than average life.

## Affirmation Number 57
## I am better than average because:

*I actively engage in the mental and emotional habits that contribute success as a lifestyle.*

As the old saying goes, “Watch your thoughts (emotions), they become your words; Watch your words, they become your actions; Watch your actions, they become your habits; Watch your habits, they become your character; Watch your character, for it becomes your destiny.”

This proverb is practically an instruction manual on how to create and live a better than average life. I take it to heart and mind and reap the rewards.

## Affirmation Number 58
## I am better than average because:

*I am focused on what is the most valuable use of my time.*

I schedule my day to maximize the efficiency of and direct the energy spent on conquering tasks and challenges that directly move me closer to my goal.

Chapter Four

# I Am Better Than Average Because of My Flock: The Team I Have Around Me

Inspirational speaker Jim Rohn famously said "You are the average of the five people you spend the most time with."

Your life up to this point is a result of the company you have kept. If you sincerely want to build and live a better than average life by being, doing and having more, you must surround yourself with people who have similar mindsets and habits and who have built and are living better than average lives of their own.

Similarly, you attract those relationships into your life in the act of paying it forward by being willing to inspire, encourage and mentor those who look to you for what they seek.

The relationships one has are as integral to creating and living a better than average life as are the goals you set, the thoughts you think and the habits you practice.

It is crucial that you intentionally build and maintain both personal and professional relationships which align with your purpose and add to, never detract from, the life you dream for yourself.

## Affirmation Number 59
## I am better than average because:

*I seek out and make myself worthy and attractive to those who can mentor, guide, support, and assist me in my journey.*

In order to achieve my goals of building and creating a better than average life I must seek out people who are successful at the things that I don't know how to do.

This is an area I will not allow fear to stop me from doing what is necessary in order to be, do and have what I want.

## Affirmation Number 60
## I am better than average because:

*I make a conscious and deliberate effort to have a minimum of 85% of my daily conversations positive, purposeful, and profitable.*

This habit of intentional conversation and company strengthens my mindset, creates possibilities and attracts more abundance and wealth in my life. This is probably the simplest way to begin building and living a better than average life.

## Affirmation Number 61
## I am better than average because:

*I insist on creating an environment in which I thrive even and especially if that means removing people close to me who are toxic.*

A better than average life is most easily created and lived in partnership with those who have common goals and ambitions. Cultivating, nurturing and strengthening those relationships is creating and living a better than average life.

## Affirmation Number 62
## I am better than average because:

*I am especially vigilant for emotional states of anger and frustration and purposely refrain spending time with people who are a constant source of pessimism or drama.*

Whether in a less than average life or a better than average life the time allotted to live either is finite. What primarily separates the two and defines either is whether that limited time is spent enjoying all that life can offer and attracting positivity back into it or being miserable because of and constantly at odds with the negativity that others create.

## Affirmation Number 63
## I am better than average because:

*I avoid low-energy people who don't encourage me to be my best.*

As I build and live a better than average life and push toward achieving my goals, I must have people in my life who recognize my ambition and potential and encourage it relentlessly rather than those who resent or minimize the better than average life I am building and living. This is just like professional athletes who employ coaches to help them reach the pinnacles of their performances.

## Affirmation Number 64
## I am better than average because:

*I deliberately gravitate to those who encourage my success.*

Most relationships are born and lived out in our comfort zones. We tend to form relationships with people who are very similar to us in their likes, dislikes, experiences, accomplishments and even levels of ambition and success.

We avoid people who challenge us to be, do, and have more and we rarely actively seek out someone who will push us and hold us accountable to doing what is required to meet or surpass our potential for success.

Building and living a better than average life is implementing and consistently practicing the same mental, emotional, spiritual, financial and other habits which successful people practice. The cast of characters in a better than average life I aspire to build and live is full of people who I can learn from, be inspired by and who encourage, advise and hold me accountable to fulfilling the requirements of the success I desire.

Because I am committed to developing and reinforcing productive and positive habits with the help of peers and mentors who express positivity as part of their successful lifestyle, I purposely form relationships with the people who will help coach me to fulfill my destiny of building and living the better than average life, which is my birthright.

## Affirmation Number 65
## I am better than average because:

*I accept the honest criticism of the people whom I admire and have more experience at that which I aspire to accomplish.*

Constructive criticism and feedback make up the blueprint for building and living a better than average life. I prefer to avoid making mistakes and improve my performance based on the input of those encouraging and personally invested in my success and who may have already overcome the obstacles I am am facing rather than having to experience those mistakes firsthand.

## Affirmation Number 66
## I am better than average because:

*I recognize, show compassion towards, help and invest in others who are committed to building and living their better than average lives by inspiring, encouraging and motivating others.*

I have faith that because I model the characteristics that I desire in the people I want around me, I will attract them into my life and be shown favor in my time of need as I strive to create and live a better than average life and help others create and live one of their own.

## Affirmation Number 67
## I am better than average because:

*I purposefully design the relationships I have with my family, friends, community and co-workers, keeping in mind I am only, but absolutely responsible for what I bring to the table.*

Better than average relationships are a necessary component of a better than average life. Holding myself accountable for contributing toward those relationships is laying the foundation for a better than average life to be built and lived.

## Affirmation Number 68
## I am better than average because:

*I am conscious of the fact that the time I spend with, is not the same as the attention I devote to the people who matter to me.*

I put away distractions when I'm around those who matter and focus on building and living a life full of better than average relationships.

## Affirmation Number 69
## I am better than average because:

*I speak to be understood and listen to understand.*

I ask questions for clarification and I make no assumptions of what isn't said nor attempt to interpret what is said to better suit my biased narrative. I actively listen to hear, process and comprehend what is being said rather than to only respond.

I think twice about what I am about to say before I say it to ensure it is necessary, truthful and accurate and unambiguous. Effective communication is the critical foundation upon which better than average relationships are built.

## Affirmation Number 70
## I am better than average because:

*I am willing to sometimes delay the payoff of accomplishment and progression toward my goals in order to assist others who require my assistance in their pursuit of a better quality of life.*

Selflessness is a critical ingredient in better than average relationships which are building blocks of better than average lives. As I help others build and live their own better than average lives I am simultaneously building and living my own by being a person who attracts the necessary support into my own life.

## Affirmation Number 71
## I am better than average because:

*I make calculated personal sacrifices of time and resources in order to aid those who are unable to compensate me or do anything that directly benefits me, simply because it is the right thing to do.*

*I do so altruistically and without judgment or expectation of recognition, reward or reimbursement.*

Though I may risk occasionally being taken for granted or advantage of I am secure in the knowledge that I earn, through karma and social capital, the ability to have whatever I want if only I help enough people get what they need.

## Affirmation Number 72
## I am better than average because:

*I am compassionate and empathic because*
*I am present.*

I am aware of the needs of the world and those around me and respond to the best of my ability. This not only creates a better than average life for myself but helps others create and live their own better than average lives.

Chapter Five

# I Am Better Than Average Because I Face My Fears and Operate Outside of My Comfort Zone

Fear is the Unforgivable Sin

Let's be honest. You have dreams and ambitions for you and your family.  You know generally, if not exactly, what you have to do to achieve the goals that you set for yourself but something stops you from taking action.

Fear.

Fear has immobilized you.

You fear how others will perceive you and what they'll say about you.

You fear the changes you'll have to make in your lifestyle.

You fear the possibility of failure. You fear leaving your

comfort zone. You fear change, criticism, and challenge.

Fear is completely natural and usually understandable, but in order to be able to build and live a better than average life and experience the happiness you long for, you cannot let these fears override `your desire for what you know is best for you.

## Affirmation Number 73
## I am better than average because:

*I am bigger than my fears, doubts, and comfort zone.*

*I refuse to allow my fears or my comfort to convince me to set small, simple goals which are unremarkable and unsatisfying.*

I don’t limit the scope of the goals which I am willing to pursue based on what I fear is unattainable or what others define as unlikely or impossible.

A better than average life is built on and lived through courage consistency and commitment to achieving success in significant ways which continue to challenge me and inspire others to do the same.

I fight for, work for, plan, build and create my success even when I'm fatigued, ill, battered and sore.

When the comfort, ease, and conformity that define an average life are tempting alternatives to achievement born from diligence and taxing efforts I chose the later because living a better than average life is my goal and creating it is my purpose.

## Affirmation Number 74
## I am better than average because:

*I operate outside of my comfort zone.*

I direct my energies toward my specific goal. I remind myself of what my motivations are for achieving the goal and I am not distracted by the lure of my comfort zone or intimidated by fear of negative outcomes.

A better than average life is built by visualizing what I most want and experienced by keeping my eye on the prize in all that I do.

## Affirmation Number 75
## I am better than average because:

*I do not compare myself or the progress I've made to others.*

My journey is mine and mine alone. It is as unique as my DNA or fingerprints. I do not expect to be as far along in the beginning of my journey as those who started before me nor do I expect to face the exact same obstacles which others have faced on my path.

The only thing that matters is that I take consistent action and hold to my commitment to doing all which is required to build and live a better than average life.

## Affirmation Number 76
## I am better than average because:

*I do not allow fear of the unknown prevent me from making tough decisions.*

For most people, fear is an emotion that motivates them to create and achieve goals so insignificant they are practically subconscious. They make safe decisions that leave them firmly planted deep inside their comfort zones.

Building and living a better than average life is about continuously growing toward my ultimate potential. True growth only comes from taking risks and seeking out discomfort.

## Affirmation Number 77
## I am better than average because:

*When it comes to accomplishing my goals, I refuse to exchange potential greatness for temporary comfort. I accept feeling unsure and insecure as part of the process, when playing it safe seems smarter, easier and comfortable.*

The better than average life that I want, deserve, and have the ability to create and live lies directly outside my comfort zone. Settling for less is counter-productive because the ultimate goal is the happiness that comes from enduring, conquering and overcoming challenges and obstacles, even my own impatience.

## Affirmation Number 78
## I am better than average because:

*I am willing to make mistakes and look foolish while searching for answers I don't yet have.*

Pride and a sense of accomplishment is what motivates me to act boldly toward achieving my goal of creating and living a better than average life rather than what dampens my ambition and keeps me tethered to a life full of mediocrity.

# Affirmation Number 79
# I am better than average because:

*I fail, reevaluate and then I begin again.*

I must remember that failure can be the most valuable weapon in my arsenal if I embrace it as an opportunity to become wiser and more valuable. The more lessons I learn from my failures the more valuable I become.

A better than average life is built and and lived through the lessons learned from trials, failures and mistakes that occur from bold action.

## Affirmation Number 80
## I am better than average because:

*I take responsibility for my actions, even when I am wrong and things turn out poorly due to my decisions.*

I do not define myself by failures so it is easy to accept responsibility for the mistakes I may make in the process of building and living a better than average life.

The lessons learned from those mistakes are the solid foundation and brick and mortar that transform that life from dreams, wishes to reality.

## Affirmation Number 81
## I am better than average because:

*I self-evaluate -- not self criticize.*

I know it is critically important that I forgive myself for both the past and future shortcomings. I remember that failing is part of the process.

The progression toward a better than average life is measured by the number of failures encountered and learned from.

## Affirmation Number 82
## I am better than average because:

*I find confidence in the fact that failures are mile markers on the road to success as long as I learn from them.*

I am not afraid to fail because each lesson learned from my failures makes me wiser and that wisdom makes me inherently more valuable.

That value is what makes my life better than average.

# Affirmation Number 83
# I am better than average because:

*I know I am only but completely*

*responsible for what I think, feel and do.*

A better than average life is built with and lived through my thoughts, emotions and actions. I build and live a better than average life by holding myself accountable to the standards that I have set for myself to do what is required to achieve my goals that satisfy my motivations.

Other people's thoughts, feelings and actions are out of my control and therefore not my responsibility to manage.

## Affirmation Number 84
## I am better than average because:

*I refuse to be weighed down by carrying that which does not belong to me.*

I only carry beliefs that serve me as I build and live a better than average life. I release burdens that are other people's drama, beliefs, limitations and expectations of me and the world which they are content to live in.

## Affirmation Number 85
## I am better than average because:

*I am not distracted by malice, unhealthy criticism.*

I remind myself that most of those who are critical of me and my decision to build and live a better than average life are the ones who are also either too lazy or afraid of making any improvements of themselves and are resentful of those who demonstrate the courage to seek more out of life. I remind myself this is their problem -- not mine.

# Affirmation Number 86
# I am better than average because:

*I don't allow anyone to mold my future by blaming them for my past or present.*

While it is extremely important to severe ties to those who do not inspire, encourage, assist, advise or hold me accountable to being a better than average person who builds and lives a better than average life, it is critical that I push myself out of the comfort zone of blaming others for my failures, mistakes, and shortcomings.

I refuse to be a victim of they, them, and their agendas.

“They did this,” or “They did that.” “They won’t give me a fair shot.” or "Because of them I wasn't able to..." is language of victims.

When I take responsibility for my mental, emotional, and behavioral habits that sabotage success or lack of or underdeveloped skills and learn the lessons they present, I am then enabled and equipped to build and live a better than average life.

## Affirmation Number 87
## I am better than average because:

*I accept complete responsibility for my success and failures.*

When I find myself in situations and circumstances that don't advance my agenda or away from my goals instead of blaming others -- I get honest with myself and ask “What did I do to contribute to the situation and what can I do next to advance toward my goal?"

Understanding what role I played in creating my circumstances allows me to honor the power I have to create new prefered conditions. Being present enough to contemplate my next best move allows me to remember any race is won, one step at a time and a better than average life is built and lived one day at a time and even moment to moment. Concentrating on making each moment, hour and day better than the last by purposefully and habitually making the next best move I naturally create and live a better than average life.

## Affirmation Number 88
## I am better than average because:

*I recognize my shortcomings as opportunities to improve, grow, and attract more opportunities.*

Because change is the goal, deliberate, managed change is a critical element to building and living a better than average life. Never do I excuse average thoughts or behavior as "just the way I am".

## Affirmation Number 89
## I am better than average because:

*I lead by example.*

*I shine my light for the world to see, by consistently doing the best I can, with what I have, in the present.*

This is my standard of behavior, not to draw attention to myself but be a beacon of inspiration for those who may be lost in the darkness of average performance and mediocrity to look toward for hope and guidance.

## Affirmation Number 90
## I am better than average because:

*I act with integrity.*

*I always do the best I can to meet and beat the expectations and standards that I have of myself even when less is required.*

This means I keep promises, meet commitments and honor responsibilities.

This covenant with the Universe attracts people into my life on whom I can depend and rely and who will assist me in creating and living a better than average life.

# Affirmation Number 91
## I am better than average because:

*I do not require an apology, permission, recognition or credit to be the best me that I can be.*

All that is required is a desire to be, a belief that I can be and a willingness to be a person who creates and lives a better than average life.

## Affirmation Number 92
## I am better than average because:

*I do not deny my talent and abilities.*

I confess and acknowledge my skills, talents, abilities and empowering habits in order to commit to using them. I speak them into existence and employ them with confidence to build and live a better than average life.

## Affirmation Number 93
## I am better than average because:

*I accept absolute responsibility for my happiness.*

This way I am more likely to make regret-proof decisions as I build and live my better than average life. I am in charge of my life and while I might not have control over every aspect of my life, I do have control over my thoughts, words, actions and character which are all the components of a better than average life.

## Affirmation Number 94
## I am better than average because:

*My ultimate aim is spiritual enlightenment.*

The material things, physical possessions, emotional peace, mental health and wisdom I desire and seek are inherent byproducts of the spiritual development which is a prerequisite of building and living a better than average life.

# Affirmation Number 95
# I am better than average because:

*I align my lifestyle with my dreams.*

I don't place limits on my goals, ambitions and desires based on my current circumstances.

The things I want aren't too expensive - I just may not be able to afford them yet.

If I set goals for what I desire, identify the obstacles, develop and implement the skills and habits necessary to overcome those obstacles and surround myself with the right people and organizations to inspire, encourage, support, advise me and hold me accountable to those goals I know I have the right and power to create new prefered circumstances..

## Affirmation Number 96
## I am better than average because:

*I choose peace. I create peace.*

The foundation of a better than average life is peace which is created through intentional, focused, managed thoughts, emotions and behaviors which I choose.

## Affirmation Number 97
## I am better than average because:

*Inner Peace is my motivation for everything I do and the gauge of all of my accomplishments.*

Wealth, fame, and all the other trappings of success are great but mean nothing without peace therefore creating and living better than average life is all about creating and living in peace.

# Affirmation Number 98
# I am better than average because:

*I am super protective of my thoughts.*

My success is shaped by the things I observe and ingest and think about. I know that regulating that to which I give my attention is critical to my success. Because the ultimate goal of creating and living a better than average life is to be happy, I intentionally do not consume or dwell unnecessarily on negativity including the news, entertainment and company I keep.

# Affirmation Number 99
# I am better than average because:

*I release others of my expectations and judgements.*

When I release my attachment to people or circumstances being a certain way for they are not within my control I am simultaneously releasing myself from unnecessary stress.

I expect success for myself and I create my prefered conditions. I hold myself accountable to those expectations and do what is necessary to create and live a better than average life.

## Affirmation Number 100
## I am better than average because:

*I act on the knowledge that forgiveness, is a prescription for inner peace.*

Holding onto grudges, remembering transgressions, being sensitive to slights and perceived acts of disrespect only generates anger, sadness and mental, emotional and spiritual turmoil. These things spoil, corrupt and sabotage a better than average life. Forgiveness helps build the foundation which a better than average life is built upon.

## Affirmation Number 101
## I am better than average because:

*My conscious is my first and most reliable guide and what I follow without question.*

Lately the title leader is often given to the loudest, most irrational, often unqualified voice which promotes a personal agenda of obtaining fame, influence and wealth by manipulating the emotions of his or her followers.

It is almost instinctually tempting to allow ourselves to align with and follow charismatic personalities who incite fear and anger by raising the alarm to implied or actual threats against our comfort zone.

This emotional manipulation often overrides rational thought and motivates the average person into blindly following and acting without contemplation, many times against their own best self interest.

A better than average life is built and lived by inspiring and being inspired to create love, peace, and unity not by inciting nor being mislead by hate, conflict and division.

**I Am Better Than Average.**

**I thoroughly appreciate you for purchasing this book.**

**I sincerely hope that you will integrate the affirmations shared in these pages to your life, so that you can achieve the success that you deserve and build and live a better than average life.**

**Thank you,**
**Jonathan McMillan**

Feel free to connect with me on the following social media sites:

Follow me on Twitter:@BTA_Jonathan

## Friend me on

Facebook: facebook.com/jonathanmcmillan

Google+: +JonathanMcMillanBeBTA

Contact me directly:
http://www.jonathanmcmillan.com/contact.html

70989812R00071

Made in the USA
San Bernardino, CA
09 March 2018